Artwork by Charlie Adlard

usually takes one to two days, depending on the remoteness of the outbreak area. During this time, the target area is surrounded by the containment team. Usually, a dozen separate bases or checkpoints are established along the major roads or at access points to the area. From these positions, constant patrols are sent in all directions to ensure no zombies are slipping through the net to infect other areas. The men on the ground

are supported by helicopters and, in some cases, unmanned drones.

As the containment is being established, a number of sorties are launched into the outbreak area with the purpose of bringing out survivors. Most of these sorties are conducted by individual fire teams on foot, though they remain in constant contact with ground and air transport, as either will be made available for emergency evacuation. These teams advance as far as they can into the zone, rounding up the living and escorting them back to the containment line. At all costs, the teams must avoid alerting and causing the movement of a horde toward the lines.

By the time the containment lines are fully established, the variety of zombie threat should have been determined. In the case of necromantics, the containment team will immediately go on the offensive, launching a massive attack from one side of the circle and attempting to overwhelm the horde with superior firepower. While the main attack goes straight after the zombies, a number of small teams attempt to infiltrate behind the lines in search of the necromancer. Most of the time the necromancer cannot be located and the mission becomes one messy clean-up operation.

Artwork by Ben Rollman

If it is determined that the zombies are either viral or atomic, a completely different strategy is employed. Instead of going on the offensive, the containment team selects a portion of its line and reinforces it with field fortifications, claymores, and emplaced weapons, setting up a defense in depth. Once this is done, a vehicle-mounted attack element is sent into the outbreak area with the specific intent of causing a zombie horde to advance toward the fortified section of the line. By baiting the zombie horde, it can be coaxed into a kill zone and wiped out by overwhelming firepower. Once the containment team destroys the main horde, it goes on the offensive, slowly collapsing the containment circle, eliminating all zombies encountered.

Most containment teams, such as the 34th, are organized to independently cope with an outbreak in a small town or village. Should the outbreak take place in a major city, or spread throughout a whole region, obviously further military aid would be needed. In this case, the general military provides the manpower to form the containment lines, while the specialist zombie hunters run sorties and handle most of the direct combat.

To date, the battle of Mexico City remains the single largest recorded zombie outbreak since the American Civil War. This battle saw the employment of

tactics similar to those described above. However, if the infection had managed to spread beyond the confines of the city, or if the number of infected had reached hundreds of thousands instead of just thousands, it is likely that such tactics would not have been effective. It remains imperative that all zombie outbreaks are contained as swiftly as possible. If the governments of the world have a plan or strategy in the event of a cataclysmic outbreak, it remains tightly under wraps. It is clear, however, that such an event would force some difficult moral decisions, that some would have to be sacrificed to save the whole. Let us pray that it never comes to that.

GLOSSARY

AGGRESSOR ZOMBIES A variety of viral zombie that is faster and
more aggressive than the normal viral zombie.

ATOMIC ZOMBIES Zombies created through chemical or
radioactive contamination of a specific geographic area.

BUREAU 9 An organization founded by Allan Pinkerton during
the American Civil War to combat the zombie threat. It continues
to function in that capacity even today.

THE "CLOAK ROOM" A secret suite of rooms hidden beneath the
British World War II codebreaking center at Bletchley Park. It
served as the Headquarters for Supreme Allied Command:
Shadow Theater (SAC:ST).

COMMAND: THE BLUE MARBLE (C:TBM) An organization
of mercenary soldiers trained as zombie hunters.

CONTAINMENT TEAMS SPECIALIST Multinational teams
within the military forces of NATO countries that can deploy
quickly to suppress zombie outbreaks.

DIVISION 77, "THE DIRGE" Zombie-containment team of the
British military.

DRAUGR Walking corpses from Norse/Viking mythology.

GRIMOIRE A book of spells or a manual for the use of black magic.

THE HONOURABLE SOCIETY OF THE RESURRECTION
MEN A group founded in 1756 in Edinburgh by an unknown
group of body-snatchers to fight the influx of necromancers in
the city.

HORDE Any gathering of at least ten zombies where they are
grouped closely enough that each member can hear the moans of
at least three other members.

IRRADIATED ZOMBIES OR "RAD ZOMBIES" The walking dead
that have been exposed to dangerous levels of radiation and now
carry that radiation inside their lifeless shell.

LICHE An undead necromancer.

THE "MOAN" A dry, warbling sound produced by some varieties
of zombies that appears to be a primitive means of
communication among them.

NECROMANCER One who uses necromancy or the magic of death.

NECROMANCY Black magic; the practice of using the dead in magical rituals.

NECROMANTIC ZOMBIES Zombies created using black magic to reanimate the bodies of the dead.

"NIGHTMEN" Nickname of the members of the US Army 34th Specialist Regiment, which specializes in zombie containment.

OPERATION EKLIPSE A World War II German mission to find certain religious artifacts, with the aim of using them to facilitate the creation of zombies in far larger numbers.

REAPER 1 AND REAPER 2 Harvester-type vehicles created to combat large groups of zombies efficiently.

REVENANTS A variety of zombie reawakened by a force that seems to come completely from within the deceased individual.

SOCIETY OF THULE A secret order founded in Munich, Germany, by a World War I veteran, devoted to the pursuit of necromantic knowledge.

SUPREME ALLIED COMMAND SHADOW THEATER (SAC:ST) A secret Allied organization formed during World War II to combat the threat of the Nazi occult program.

TODESRITTER ("DEATH KNIGHTS") A unit of zombie soldiers unleashed by Hitler during World War II.

VIRAL HOUNDS Zombie canines.

VIRAL ZOMBIES Zombies created through a contagious virus that infects the living and turns them into zombies, following the rapid onset of death.

VOODOO A magical and religious practice, often involving witchcraft and necromancy, largely centered in the islands of the Caribbean Sea

VOODOO ZOMBIE A particular form of necromantic zombie created through the use of voodoo.

Z-VIRUS The virus that creates zombies.

THE ZOMBIE DUELING ASSOCIATION An underground gladiatorial society which pits captured zombies against hired gladiators.

ZOMBIE HUNTERS Those who hunt down and try to eliminate the threat represented by zombies.

ZOMBIE MASTER A term once applied to necromancers who had assembled a large force of zombie minions, but has recently become more commonly associated with a zombie Typhoid Mary: a living human who carries the zombie virus and can transmit it to others without suffering its effects.

FOR MORE INFORMATION

American Society for Psychical Research, Inc. (ASPR)
5 West 73rd Street
New York, NY 10023
(212) 799-5050
Web site: http://www.aspr.com
This organization's mission is to explore extraordinary or unexplained phenomena
   that have been called psychic or paranormal and their implications for our
   understanding of consciousness, the universe, and the nature of existence. It
   addresses questions with scientific research and offers educational activities
   including lectures and conferences.

Ghost Hunters
Syfy Channel
NBCUniversal Cable Entertainment Group
30 Rockefeller Plaza
New York, NY - 10112
(212) 664-4444
http://www.syfy.com/ghosthunters
In each episode of the *Ghost Hunters* television program, Jason Hawes and his team
   of paranormal investigators, TAPS (The Atlantic Paranormal Society) investigate
   paranormal activity across the country.

Parapsychological Association, Inc. (PA)
PO Box 24173
Columbus, OH 43224
(202) 318-2364
Web site: http://www.parapsych.org
The Parapsychological Association is the international professional organization of
   scientists and scholars engaged in the study of "psi" (or "psychic") experiences,
   such as telepathy, clairvoyance, and psychic healing. The PA endorses no
   ideologies or beliefs other than the value of rigorous scientific and scholarly
   inquiry.

Rhine Research Center
2741 Campus Walk Avenue
Building 500
Durham, NC 27705
(919) 309-4600
Web site: http://rhinecenter.org
The Rhine Research Center's mission is to advance the science of
    parapsychology, to provide education and resources for the public and
    to foster a community for individuals with personal and professional
    interest in paranormal phenomena and the nature of human
    consciousness.

Websites

Because of the changing nature of internet links, Rosen Publishing has
developed an online list of websites related to the subject of this book.
This site is updated regularly. Please use this link to access the list:

http://www.rosenlinks.com/MH/zombies

For Further Reading

Brooks, Max, and Ibraim Roberson. *The Zombie Survival Guide: Recorded Attacks.* New York, NY: Three Rivers Press, 2009.

Buckland, Raymond. *The Weiser Field Guide to Ghosts: Apparitions, Spirits, Spectral Lights, and Other Hauntings of History and Legend.* San Francisco, CA: Weiser Books, 2009.

Curran, Bob. *Encyclopedia of the Undead: A Field Guide to Creatures That Cannot Rest in Peace.* Franklin Lakes, NJ: New Page Books, 2006.

Curran, Bob. *Werewolves: A Field Guide to Shapeshifters, Lycanthropes, and Man-Beasts.* Franklin Lakes, NJ: New Page Books, 2009.

Inguanzo, Ozzy. *Zombies on Film: The Definitive Story of Undead Cinema.* New York, NY: Rizzoli, 2014.

Konstantinos. *Werewolves: The Occult Truth.* Woodbury, MN: Llewellyn Publications, 2010.

Krulos, Tea. *Monster Hunters: On the Trail with Ghost Hunters, Bigfooters, Ufologists, and Other Paranormal Investigators.* Chicago, IL: Chicago Review, 2015.

Ma, Roger. *The Vampire Combat Manual: A Guide To Fighting the Bloodthirsty Undead.* New York, NY: Berkeley Books, 2012.

Ma, Roger. *The Zombie Combat Manual.* New York, NY: Berkley Books, 2010.

Mogk, Matt. *Everything You Ever Wanted to Know About Zombies.* New York, NY: Gallery Books, 2011.

Peck, M. Scott. *Glimpses of the Devil: A Psychiatrist's Personal Accounts of Possession, Exorcism, and Redemption.* New York, NY: Free Press, 2009.

Schwalb, Suzanne, and Margaret Rubiano. *Vampires, Werewolves, Zombies: Compendum Monstrum: From the Papers of Herr Doktor Max Sturm & Baron Ludwig Von Drang.* White Plains, NY: Peter Pauper Press, 2010.

Schlozman, Steven C., and Andrea Sparacio. *The Zombie Autopsies: Secret Notebooks From the Apocalypse.* New York, NY: Grand Central, 2012.

INDEX

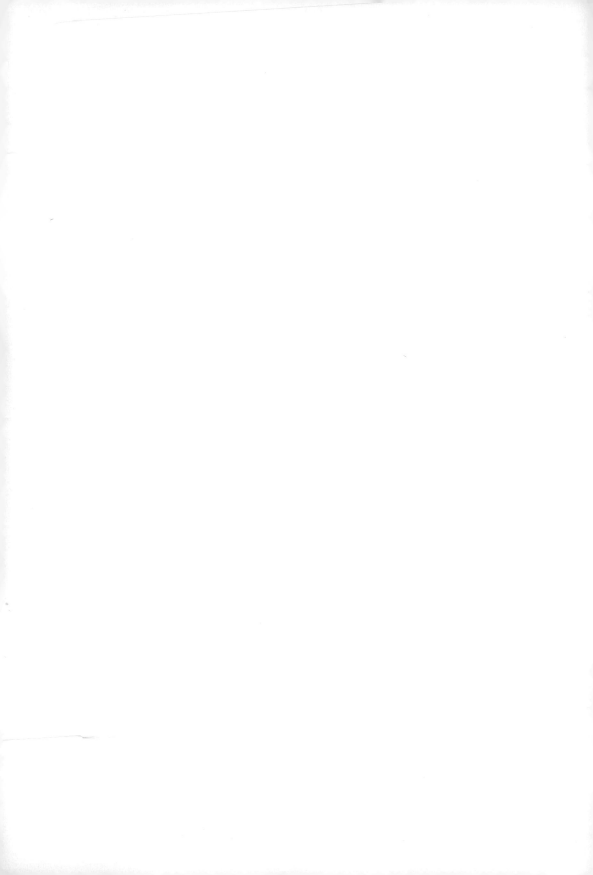

Using Scientific Tools

AUTHOR
SUSAN
MARKOWITZ
MEREDITH

ROURKE PUBLISHING

Vero Beach, Florida 32964

www.rourkepublishing.com

PHOTO CREDITS:© S-E-R-G-O: p. 4, 5, 10, 11, 22, 23, 36, 37, 42, 43, 46, 47; © bubaone: p. 4, 5, 10, 11, 22, 23, 36, 37, 42, 43, 46, 47; © geopaul: p. 4, 5, 10, 11, 22, 23, 36, 37, 42, 43, 46, 47; © P. Wei: p. 5, 7; © Jaimie D. Travis: p. 5; © annfoto: p. 5;© Nick Schlax: p. 5; © Julián Rovagnati: p. 5; © marcio eugenio: p. 6; © Stephan Morris: p. 7; © Ivan Kmit: p. 7; © Matjaz Boncina: p. 7; © Stefan Ataman: p. 7; © Yannis Ntousiopoulos: p. 7; © Karen Mower: p. 7; © ungorf: p. 7; © Bart Coenders: p. 8; © Murat Giray Kaya: p. 9; © eva serrabassa: p. 9; © Lisa Gagne: p. 10; © 4x6: p. 11; © Steve Firmender: p. 12, 13; © james benet: p. 14; © Stephan Hoerold: p. 14,15; © Grafissimo: p. 16; © Jacom Stephans: p. 19; © narvikk: p. 20; © Graffizone: p. 20; © Free Styler Photo: p. 21; © Milos Luzanin: p. 22; © kate_sept2004: p. 23; © blackred: p. 24; © Step2626: p. 25; © Tatiana Popova: p. 25; © Emrah Turudu: p. 25; © Sinisa Botas: p. 26; © Wikipedia: p. 27; © Rafael Laguillo: p. 28; © DNY59: p. 29; © Murat Koc: p. 31; © Mischa Gossen: p. 31; © Elena Korenbaum: p. 33; © Ashok Rodrigues: p. 34; © Pamela Moore: p. 35; © Jose Gil: p. 36; © Radu Razvan: p. 38; © Frank Boston: p. 39; © Marcy Smith: p. 40; © 3DProfi: p. 41; © Laurence Gough: p. 43; © Paul Gardner: p. 44; © Mara Rideva: p. 45;

Edited by Kelli L. Hicks

Cover and Interior design by Teri Intzegian

Library of Congress Cataloging-in-Publication Data

Meredith, Susan Markowitz.
 Using scientific tools / Susan Markowitz Meredith.
   p. cm. -- (Let's explore science)
 Includes index.
 ISBN 978-1-60694-413-4 (hard cover)
 ISBN 978-1-60694-531-5 (soft cover)
 1. Scientific apparatus and instruments--Juvenile literature. I. Title.
 Q185.3.M464 2010
 502.8--dc22

                              2009005739

Printed in the USA

CG/CG

ROURKE PUBLISHING

www.rourkepublishing.com - rourke@rourkepublishing.com
Post Office Box 643328 Vero Beach, Florida 32964

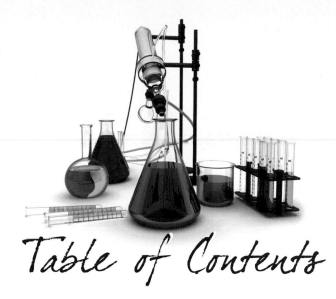

Table of Contents

CHAPTER ONE

Using Tools in Science

We all use tools to get things done. To eat soup, we use a spoon. To move a heavy box, we use a cart. To sign our name, we use a pen. Every tool, large or small, exists to do a job.

DID YOU KNOW?

Tools have been helping people throughout history. Spears and arrows aided ancient hunters. Early farmers made use of simple plows. For writing, people once used hollow reeds and wing feathers.

Tools Extend Us

Tools allow us to do things beyond our natural abilities. Some tools extend our physical strength, our reach, and our speed. Other tools expand the limits of our senses. Still others provide us with added brain power.

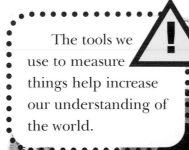

The tools we use to measure things help increase our understanding of the world.

The Right Tool

Without the right tool, many tasks are difficult or impossible. But a useful tool can inspire people to use it in various ways. One tool is not suited for all purposes, though. So inventors are always designing new and better tools for specific jobs.

Scientific knowledge contributes to the invention of some tools. The light bulb, for instance, would not exist

DID YOU KNOW?

The term **technology** applies to any practical use of scientific knowledge. Many nations are technologically advanced because the lifestyles of their citizens depend on technology.

without knowledge of electricity. Likewise, earlier scientific discoveries made engines, televisions, and microwave ovens possible.

PAST TO PRESENT

TELEVISION

TV networks send television signals through the air at the speed of light. Today, all TV signals in the United States are a digital signal.

PAST

PRESENT

PAST

PRESENT

MUSIC PLAYER

Audiotapes store music as magnetioc signals. Compact discs (CDs) and digital files store it as data. All music players convert stored material back into sound.

LIGHT BULB

All light bulbs use electric power to produce light. The latest types of bulbs have been improved to use less electricity to produce light.

PAST

PRESENT

PRESENT

CELL PHONE

Every cell phone uses radio waves to send and receive messages. Voice, text, picture, and video messages are common on today's cell phones.

PAST

Scientific Tools Everywhere

Scientists, both young and old, use tools to help them find or discover information. From the simplest to the most advanced, tools are useful at every stage of the scientific **process**. Certain tools are ideal for observing and collecting information. Scientists rely on other tools to conduct experiments. To organize and store data, and share it with others, scientists make use of an even different set of tools.

Wherever investigations into science take place, tools are in use. In laboratories, biologists use powerful instruments to study cells. Chemists use other devices to analyze substances. In the field, special tools allow geologists to explore the Earth and astronomers to study the stars.

BIOLOGIST

ASTRONOMER

CHEMIST

100 ml

250m

CHAPTER TWO

Tools That Extend the Senses

We use our senses to observe everything around us. For some scientists, though, that is not enough. They rely on tools that go far beyond what their own senses can take in.

Binoculars, which are handheld, are two telescopes side-by-side.

Observing Far Away

Telescopes make distant objects such as planets and stars seem bigger and closer. The **optical** telescope is the most common type. Just like our eyes, this telescope makes use of light.

In the early 1600's, Dutchman Hans Lippershey probably made the first optical telescope. Nearby in Italy, Galileo Galilei built and used a similar telescope to explore the sky.

Types of Telescopes

There are several types of optical telescopes. The most common is a **refracting** telescope. It has a long tube-like shape. At one end is a large curved piece of glass, called an **objective** lens. It collects light waves from distant objects. The lens works by slowing down the light waves passing through it. These waves take longer to go through its thick middle. As a result, all the different light waves reach the same point on the far side of the lens at the same time. This point is the focus and a detailed image forms.

viewfinder

eyepiece

A refracting telescope also has a small lens in the eyepiece. It allows the user to see the image even more clearly.

focus knob

star diagonal prism inside here

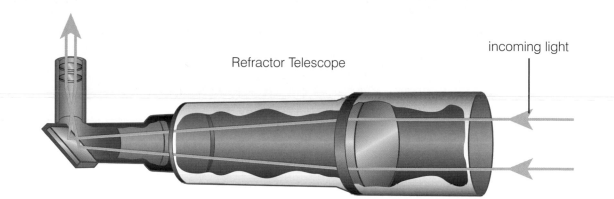

Refractor Telescope

incoming light

projective ring
prevents glare on lens

wingnut
holds telescope
body steady

objective lens
inside here

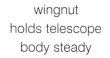

main telescope body

The objective
lens in a refracting
telescope has a **convex**
shape. Its curve looks like
the outside of a sphere.

altazimuth mount
allows horizontal and
vertical movement

tripod leg

The English scientist Isaac Newton was first to build a telescope with a mirror instead of a lens. The year was 1668. Today, most large telescopes use mirrors.

This type of optical telescope is a **reflecting** telescope. The main mirror has a bowl shape. It reflects all the light waves that hit it. The mirror's shape forces the various waves to reach the same focus point at the same time. A smaller mirror reflects the waves again to an eyepiece, or to an image-making device.

DID YOU KNOW?

The Hubble Space Telescope is a powerful reflecting telescope that orbits the Earth. The images it forms are highly detailed. They are sharper than images coming from telescopes on the ground.

Many large optical telescopes are housed in remote **observatories**. The Keck Observatory, for instance, sits on a volcanic mountain in Hawaii. Each of its two optical telescopes uses a huge reflecting mirror.

Other types of telescopes pick up different waves from objects in space. Such waves include radio, ultraviolet, and infrared waves—even x-rays.

The Keck Observatory is 8 stories tall and weights 300 tons!

Observing Close Up

A magnifying glass is a lens that makes objects look bigger than they really are. But it can only enlarge something 10 to 20 times (10x to 20x). Microscopes, on the other hand, can make objects look hundreds or thousands of times larger. The optical, or light, microscope is the most common type.

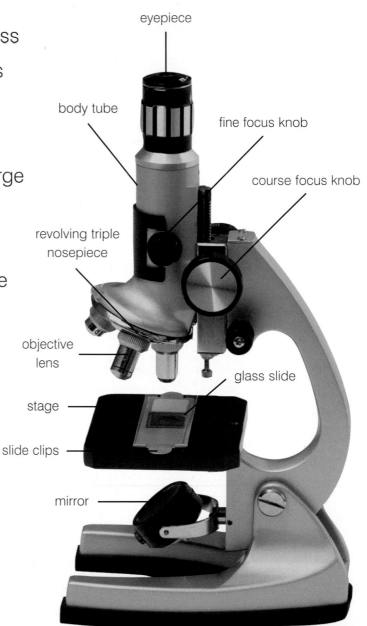

eyepiece

body tube

fine focus knob

course focus knob

revolving triple nosepiece

objective lens

glass slide

stage

slide clips

mirror

How an Optical Microscope Works

PARTS OF MICROSCOPE	USES
specimen, slide, stage, and mirror	The specimen on the glass slide rests on the stage. The mirror below reflects light up through the hole in the stage. The user adjusts the mirror to direct more or less light through the specimen.
nosepiece	The nosepiece holds lens systems, or objectives. Each objective magnifies the specimen a different amount. The user rotates the nosepiece to choose an objective. Microscopes with two or more objectives are compound microscopes.
eyepiece	The eyepiece contains a lens that further enlarges the image formed by the objective lens. The user adjusts the focus by turning the coarse and fine knobs.

Other Optical Microscopes

Some optical microscopes do not gather light all at once. Instead, they scan the specimen with a laser beam, spot by spot. A special device measures the light coming from each spot. A computer then uses this data to display an image on the monitor.

Waves Shorter Than Light

To magnify a specimen even more, scientists often use an **electron microscope**. It forms images by using tiny electron beams rather than light waves. Some electron microscopes show detail less than one angstrom apart. An **angstrom** equals 1/10,000,000 millimeter (1/254,000,000 inch).

An electron microscope reveals
amazing detail in this tiny ant.

Today's high-powered
optical microscopes magnify
a specimen up to 2,000 times. The
earliest single-lens microscopes, made
by Dutch scientist Anton van
Leeuwenhoek, magnified no more than
270 times.

*This electron microscope's beams are less than one
angstrom in length. They are about 4,000 times
smaller than the shortest visible light waves.*

Recording Sights and Sounds

Scientists who want to record what they see and hear use many devices. A camcorder is a commonly used tool for recording picture and sound together. This battery-powered machine has a built-in microphone. Some camcorders record onto magnetic tape. Newer models use memory cards.

Memory cards are ideal to store images from a small camera.

Many other types of recording devices are in use today. High-speed cameras, for instance, let researchers observe various processes in slow motion. Other cameras allow scientists to shoot unnoticed at night. Still others operate deep in the ocean.

Underwater cameras must be completely waterproof.

Listening to Animals

Special audio equipment is useful in picking up **infrasonic sounds**. These sounds are too low-pitched for human ears to hear. Low-pitched sound waves vibrate very slowly. Elephants often produce infrasonic sounds.

Medical doctors use machines that send **ultrasound** waves into the body. These sound waves are so high-pitched that human ears can't hear them. An ultrasound machine converts the echoes of these fast vibrating waves into an image. Using this technique, a doctor can see a fetus inside a mother's womb.

Scientists using infrasonic sound devices have learned that elephants communicate long distances with their deep calls.

CHAPTER THREE

Measurement Tools

An object's size and weight are both measurable. We can also measure such things as how far, how much, and how hot or cold. Even when and where are measurable. Although these measurements are different from one another, they all have something in common. Each one relates to a specific set of units that people have agreed upon.

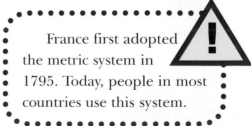

France first adopted the metric system in 1795. Today, people in most countries use this system.

The Metric System

The metric system is a group of measurement units. All of its units, large and small, are built by using multiples of 10.

This system is very useful to scientists because each unit is connected. For instance, the base unit of length is the meter. A kilometer equals 1,000 meters. Likewise, a kilogram equals 1,000 grams. Grams are the units used to measure weight.

DID YOU KNOW?

In the United States, people commonly use the customary units of measure, rather than metric. Inches, feet, yards, and miles are the units for measuring length. Ounces and pounds are for measuring weight. Volume is in cups, pints, quarts, and gallons. There is no common system to connect these various units.

Measuring Temperature

A thermometer is an instrument for measuring temperatures of different gases, liquids, and solids. There are many types of thermometers. One common type is the thermal expansion thermometer.

Thermal expansion thermometers have a long glass tube with a bulb at the base. Sealed inside the tube is liquid mercury. When the temperature goes up, the mercury expands and rises up the tube. When the temperature gets lower, the mercury contracts. The mercury sinks back down.

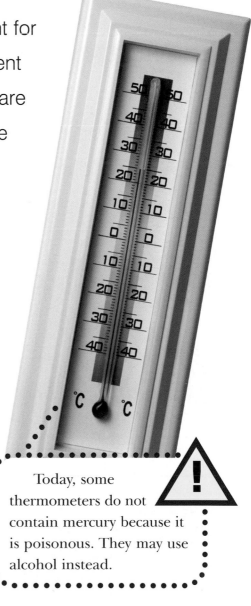

Today, some thermometers do not contain mercury because it is poisonous. They may use alcohol instead.

The marks on the outside of the tube are the temperature scale. This scale gives a value to the mercury's changing height. The value, or mark, relates to the scale used.

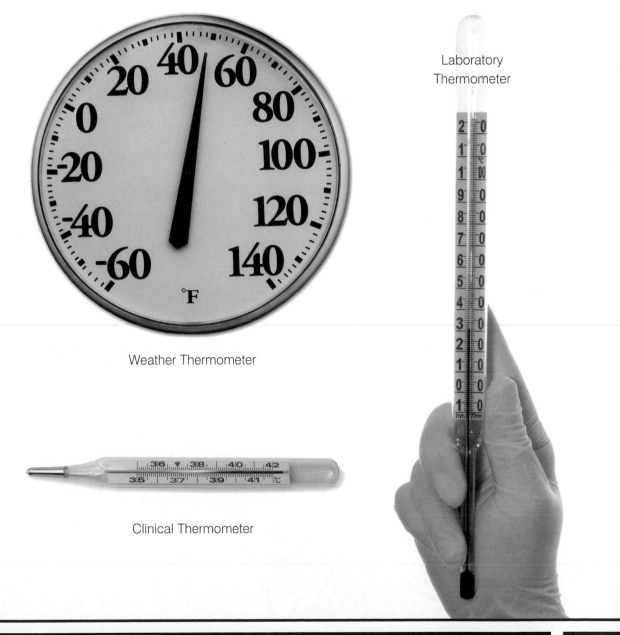

Laboratory
Thermometer

Weather Thermometer

Clinical Thermometer

Different Temperature Scales

Some thermometers use two different temperature scales: Celsius and Fahrenheit. Anders Celsius and Gabriel Fahrenheit were their creators. Both men lived in the 1700's.

The two most important points on these scales are the freezing point and boiling point of water. The Celsius scale makes 0° the point at which water freezes. Water's boiling point is 100° on this scale. The difference between the two points is 100°. The Fahrenheit scale makes 32° as water's freezing point and 212° as its boiling point. The difference between the two points is 180°.

Scientists around the world use the Celsius scale. Its 100-point system fits in with the metric system.

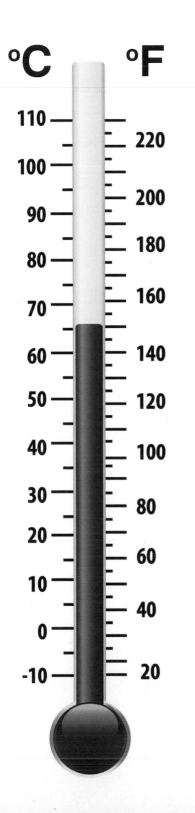

°C

110 —
100 —
90 —
80 —
70 —
60 —
50 —
40 —
30 —
20 —
10 —
0 —
-10 —

°F

— 220
— 200
— 180
— 160
— 140
— 120
— 100
— 80
— 60
— 40
— 20

DID YOU KNOW?

British physicist Lord Kelvin thought there was a limit to how cold something could get. In the 1800's he created a temperature scale based on the idea that an absolute zero exists. Absolute zero, or 0°, in the Kelvin scale is the same as -273.15°C or -459.67°F.

The Celsius and Fahrenheit scales differ in the units used to measure the mercury's rise and fall.

Measuring Weight

Weighing devices have been around a long time. The earliest type, called a balance, was popular in ancient Egypt 4,500 years ago. Even today, scientists use balances for weighing light materials.

The two pan balance is one of many different types of balance scales.

Using an Equal~Arm Balance

This type of balance is useful in making sure that two materials weigh the same. It has a horizontal bar that holds a hanging pan at each end. The user places one material with a known weight in the first pan. The other material goes in the second pan. If the first pan is heavier, it will drop down.

To reach an equal weight, the user adds more material to the second pan. Eventually, neither pan drops lower than the other. Usually a pointer shows if the pans are balanced. If so, the materials weigh the same amount.

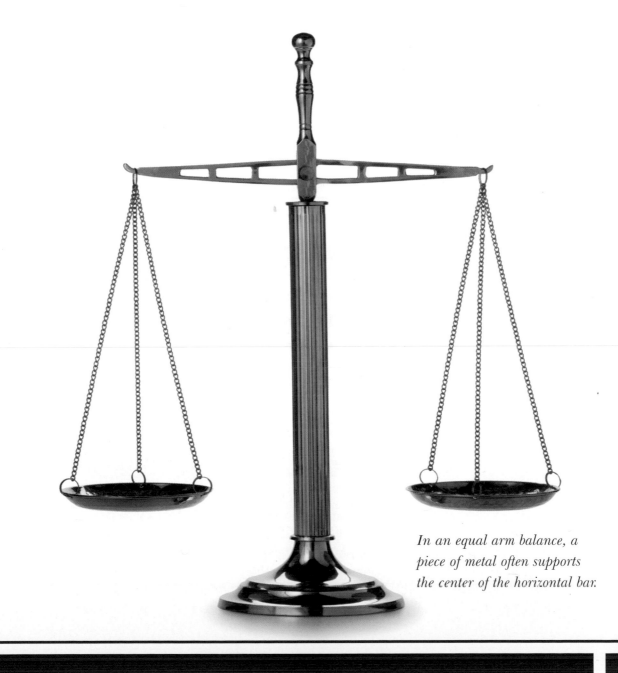

In an equal arm balance, a piece of metal often supports the center of the horizontal bar.

Triple Beam Balance

Another common weighing device is the triple beam balance. This mechanical scale weighs objects differently. However, it is still a balance because its job is to balance different weights.

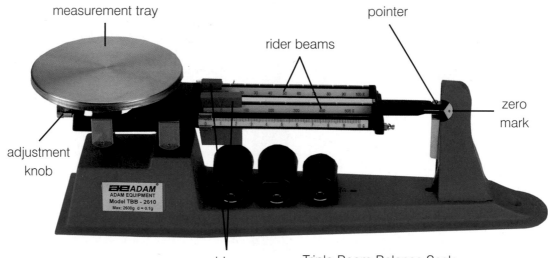

measurement tray

pointer

rider beams

zero mark

adjustment knob

riders

Triple Beam Balance Scale

TRY THIS!!!

STEP 1	STEP 2	STEP 3
To weigh something, the user first slides the three moveable weights (called poises, or riders) to the left side of the beams. The pointer should be at the zero mark on the scale.	Then the user places the object in the pan. The pointer will move away from zero. By moving the two heavier weight riders, then the lightest one, to the correct positions, the pointer will return to zero. Now the load is balanced.	To read the object's weight in grams, the user adds up the three numbers marked by the riders.

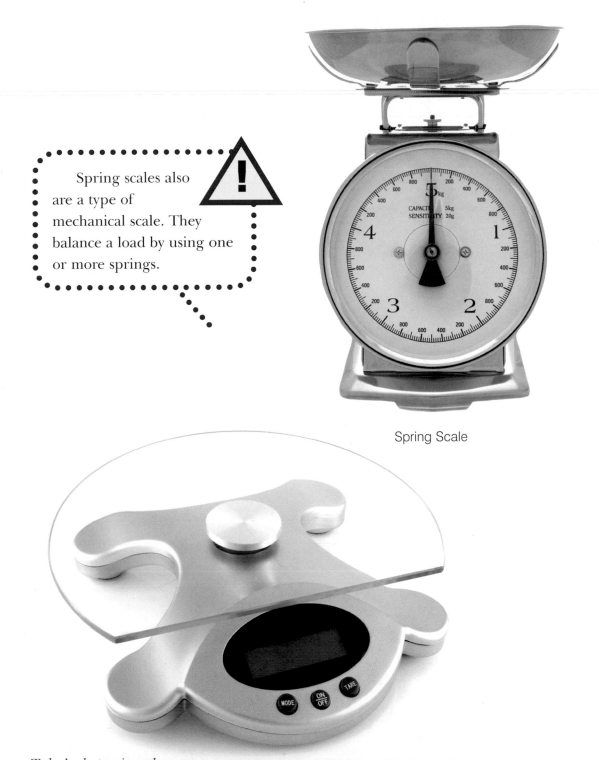

Spring scales also are a type of mechanical scale. They balance a load by using one or more springs.

Spring Scale

Today's electronic scales weigh objects very precisely.

Electronic Scale

In the Laboratory

Scientists do a lot of work in the lab. There, they can carefully study objects and materials gathered in the field. The lab is also a useful place for conducting experiments and testing out ideas.

Typical Lab Tools

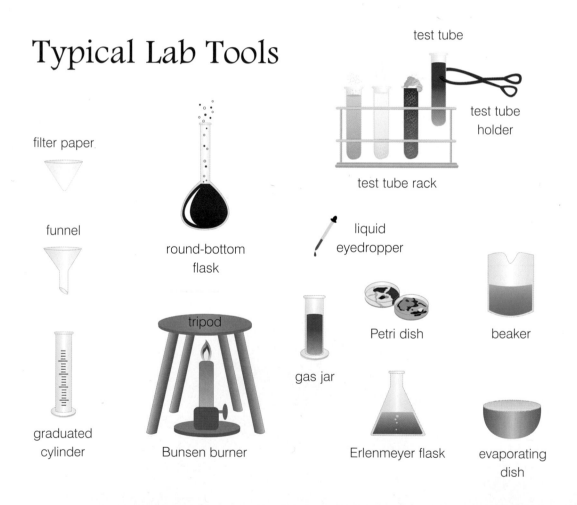

test tube

test tube holder

test tube rack

filter paper

funnel

round-bottom flask

liquid eyedropper

Petri dish

beaker

graduated cylinder

tripod

gas jar

Bunsen burner

Erlenmeyer flask

evaporating dish

What Makes Up a Mixture?

When scientists want to study the parts of a mixture, they need advanced equipment. One machine called a **centrifuge** separates liquid mixtures.

Centrifuges spin from 800 to 6,000 times per minute.

It also separates solids within a liquid. The centrifuge does its job by rotating the containers that hold the mixtures. This causes the different substances to move apart. Each has a different **density**.

Lab Safety

Laboratory work often involves chemicals, glass, and open flames. That's why it helps to follow safety procedures. Scientists of all ages learn how to set up lab equipment, and use it properly. They also have training in how to conduct experiments in a careful, step-by-step way. This ensures safety in the lab and that results from experiments are not accidental.

ADVICE!!!
IN HANDLING GLASSWARE:

- Pick up hot glassware with tongs or heat-protective gloves.
- Avoid handling broken glass.
- Don't use chipped, cracked, or dirty glassware.
- Never place hot glassware in cold water.

Accidents happen in the lab. So it's helpful to know where safety equipment is stored. Knowing the location of the fire alarm and emergency exit are important, too.

Chemistry Experiments

Scientists working with chemicals know that these materials can be dangerous. To limit the danger, chemists read all labels. They also know how to dispose of chemicals and transfer them from place to place.

CHAPTER FOUR

Models as Tools

Scientists often use words to explain their findings. But presenting ideas in a visual way is sometimes more effective. Such visual models represent a real object or process. Models may even explain a law of nature.

Some models are two-dimensional (2D), while others are three-dimensional (3D). Other models may move in some way. Whatever type of model, it can serve as a tool for understanding.

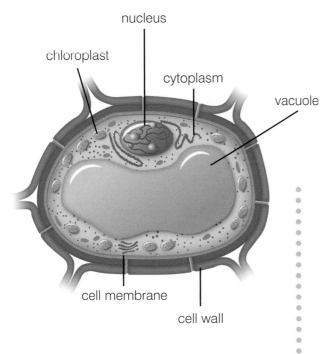

nucleus

chloroplast

cytoplasm

vacuole

cell membrane

cell wall

PHYSICAL MODELS

This is a model of Earth, from its outer crust to inner core.

This model shows the structure of a typical plant cell.

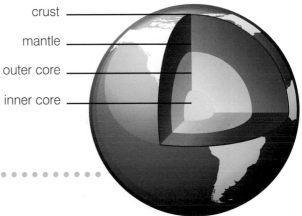

crust

mantle

outer core

inner core

Solar system models often have moveable parts.

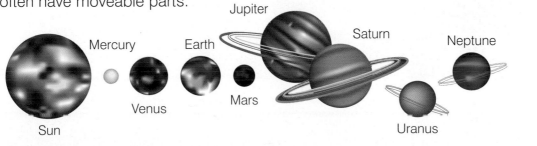

Jupiter

Mercury

Earth

Saturn

Neptune

Venus

Mars

Sun

Uranus

Models of How Things Work

Various natural cycles and laws of nature are often hard to grasp. They may be very complex. Models can help make these concepts more understandable.

Scientific models are not perfect. They cannot show every detail of an object or cycle. They often change as scientists make new discoveries.

TWO-DIMENSIONAL

Water Cycle Model

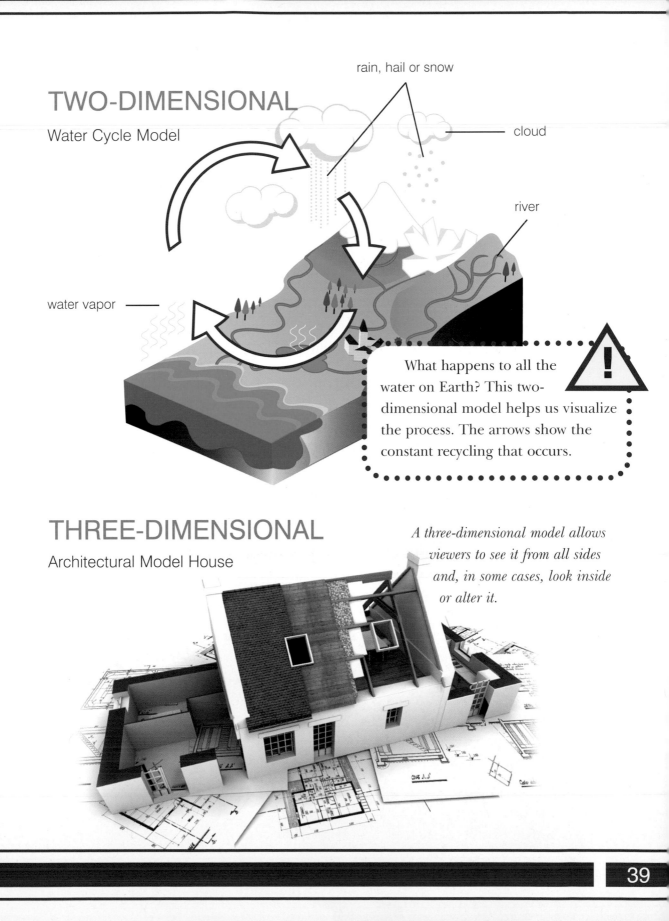

rain, hail or snow

cloud

river

water vapor

What happens to all the water on Earth? This two-dimensional model helps us visualize the process. The arrows show the constant recycling that occurs.

THREE-DIMENSIONAL

Architectural Model House

A three-dimensional model allows viewers to see it from all sides and, in some cases, look inside or alter it.

Computer Models

Computers make new types of models possible. Scientists can build computer models that are viewable at different angles, and at different layers. Also, models can show natural processes of all kinds in a step-by-step manner.

The question at the heart of some computer models is, what if? What would happen if this or that condition changed? How would it affect the model? This type of changeable model is a computer **simulation**. Scientists of all ages make use of computer simulations.

How does an ecosystem respond to different conditions? How does a building stand up to earthquakes? These are examples of computer simulations.

CHAPTER FIVE

Scientific Tools Are Changing

Young scientists are eager to test their ideas.

Scientific knowledge is growing everyday. As a result, new technology is developing all the time. This technology often improves our lives in some way. But this same technology can also open new doors for scientists. Many of them make use of the latest tools to explore their ideas. Their new discoveries can give rise to new technology.

Computer Technology

Computer technology got its start in the 1940's. The earliest computers were so large they took up whole rooms. But scientific knowledge led to advances in the technology. Today, computing devices are millions of times smaller. But they are more powerful and faster than ever.

This scientist uses a computer to keep track of her findings.

⚠ Scientists use different types of computers at different times. Whatever the work, a scientist depends on the computer's speed and **accuracy** to get the job done.

Tiny Technology

A new technology is quietly entering our day-to-day lives. It is a technology of the very tiny. Its name is **nanotechnology**. Nano means billionth. One nanometer is 1 billionth of a meter (1/25,400,000 inch). Scientists and engineers are now using this technology to make products and materials.

Today, manufacturers use nano particles in some packaging to keep food from spoiling.

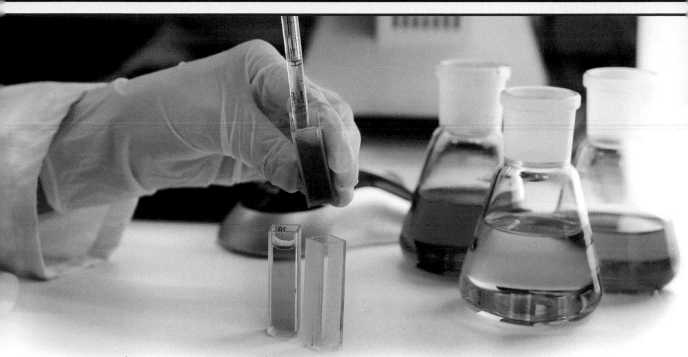

Tools are Tools

Nanotechnology will be a major tool of the future. Already, some scientists use nano particles to speed up chemical reactions. Other researchers use nano tubes to conduct electricity. Nano devices can even act as sensors. As the technology improves, these tiny tools will be able to do things never done before.

But even the most advanced scientific tools have something in common with the simplest ones. They all exist to do a job. And that job is to help scientists better understand the world we live in.

accuracy (AK-yuh-ruh-see): being careful and exact

angstrom (ANG-strum): 1/10,000,000 millimeter (1/254,000,000 inch)

centrifuge (SEN-trif-yooj): a spinning machine that separates substances of different densities

chromatograph (KROH-muh-to-grahf): a device that separates substances by pushing them through a material that absorbs each substance at a different rate.

convex (KON-veks): curved outward, like the outside of a sphere

density (DEN-si-tee): how light or heavy something is for its size

electron microscope (i-LEK-tron MYE-kruh-skope): a type of microscope that uses electron beams instead of light waves

infrasonic sound (IN-fruh-son-ik SOUND): below the pitch that humans can hear

nanotechnology (NA-no-tek-NOL-uh-jee): the careful handling of the smallest amount of a substance, such as molecules and atoms, to build larger structures

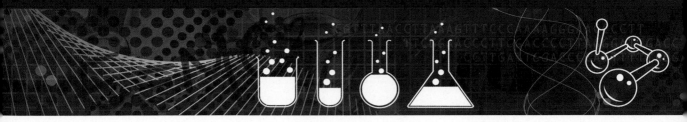

optical (OP-tuh-kuhl): to do with eyesight

objective (uhb-JEK-tiv): another name for the lens in a telescope or microscope

observatories (ohb-ZUR-vuh-tor-ees): buildings that contain telescopes and other equipment used to study the sky

process (PROSS-ess): a step-by-step group of actions that have a result

reflecting (re-FLECT-ing): bouncing off

refracting (ri-FRAKT-ing): bending or changing direction

simulation (sim-yuh-LA-shuhn): a copy or imitation of something

technology (tek-NOL-uh-jee): scientific knowledge used for making practical things

ultrasound (UHL-truh-sound): sound so high-pitched that human ears can't hear it.

Index

Websites to Visit

amazing-space.stsci.edu

www.billnye.com

news.nationalgeographic.com/news/2008/12/photogalleries/
  best-microscopic-life-photos/index.html

www.sciencenewsforkids.org

About the Author

Susan Markowitz Meredith likes to learn about the nature of things. She especially enjoys sharing what she discovers with young readers. So far, she has written 40 books on a variety of topics, including natural and physical science. Ms. Meredith also has produced quite a few TV shows for young thinkers.